# Saint Gerard

*Novena and Prayers*

———————❦———————

**Pauline**
BOOKS & MEDIA
Boston

Nihil Obstat:     Rev. John J. Connelly, S.T.D.

Imprimatur:    ✠ Bernard Cardinal Law
               Archbishop of Boston
               July 5, 2001

ISBN 0-8198-7058-7

Cover art: Anna Lewila

Texts of the New Testament used in this work are taken from *The St. Paul Catholic Edition of the New Testament*, translated by Mark A. Wauck. Copyright © 1992, Society of St. Paul. All rights reserved.

Texts of the Psalms used in this work are translated by Manuel Miguens. Copyright © 1995, Daughters of St. Paul.

All other Old Testament Scripture quotations are from the Holy Bible, *New International Version*. Copyright © 1973, 1978, 1984 International Bible Society. Used by permission of Zondervan Bible Publishers.

"P" and "Pauline" are registered trademarks of the Daughters of St. Paul.

Copyright © 2002, Daughters of St. Paul

Published by Pauline Books & Media, 50 Saint Pauls Avenue, Boston MA 02130-3491. www.pauline.org.

Printed in the U.S.A.

Pauline Books & Media is the publishing house of the Daughters of St. Paul, an international congregation of women religious serving the Church with the communications media.

5 6 7 8 9 10                                              17 16 15 14 13

# Contents

# What Is a Novena?

The Catholic tradition of praying novenas has its roots in the earliest days of the Church. In the Acts of the Apostles we read that after the ascension of Jesus, the apostles returned to Jerusalem, to the upper room, where "They all devoted themselves single-mindedly to prayer, along with some women and Mary the Mother of Jesus and his brothers" (Acts 1:14). Jesus had instructed his disciples to wait for the coming of the Holy Spirit, and on the day of Pentecost, the Spirit of the Lord came to them. This prayer of the first Christian community was the first "novena." Based on this, Christians have always prayed for various needs, trusting that God both hears and answers prayer.

The word "novena" is derived from the Latin term *novem*, meaning nine. In biblical times numbers held deep symbolism for people. The number "three," for example, symbolized perfection, fullness, completeness. The number nine—three times

5

three—symbolized perfection times perfection. Novenas developed because it was thought that—symbolically speaking—nine days represented the perfect amount of time to pray. The ancient Greeks and Romans had the custom of mourning for nine days after a death. The early Christian Church offered Mass for the deceased for nine consecutive days. During the Middle Ages novenas in preparation for solemn feasts became popular, as did novenas to particular saints.

Whether a novena is made solemnly—in a parish church in preparation for a feastday—or in the privacy of one's home, as Christians we never really pray alone. Through the waters of Baptism we have become members of the body of Christ and are thereby united to every other member of Christ's Mystical Body. When we pray, we are spiritually united with all the other members.

Just as we pray for each other while here on earth, those who have gone before us and are united with God in heaven can pray for us and intercede for us as well. We Catholics use the term "communion of saints" to refer to this exchange of spiritual help among the members of the Church on earth, those who have died and are being purified, and the saints in heaven.

While nothing can replace the celebration of Mass and the sacraments as the Church's highest form of prayer, devotions have a special place in Catholic life. Devotions such as the Stations of the Cross can help us enter into the sufferings of Jesus and give us an understanding of his personal love for us. The mysteries of the rosary can draw us into meditating on the lives of Jesus and Mary. Devotions to the saints can help us witness to our faith and encourage us in our commitment to lead lives of holiness and service as they did.

---

## How to use this booklet

The morning and evening prayers are modeled on the Liturgy of the Hours, following its pattern of psalms, scripture readings and intercessions.

We suggest that during the novena you make time in your schedule to pray the morning prayer and evening prayer. If you are able, try to also set aside a time during the day when you can pray the novena and any other particular prayer(s) you have chosen. Or you can recite the devotional prayers at the conclusion of the morning or evening prayer. What is important is to pray with expectant faith and confidence in a loving God who will answer our prayers in the way that will most benefit us. The Lord "satisfies the thirsty, and the hungry he fills with good things" (Ps 107:9).

# St. Gerard

*W*hen Gerard was born on April 6, 1726, in the Italian village of Muro, he seemed so frail that his parents, Dominic and Benedetta Majella, had him baptized immediately. But Gerard survived and grew up as a happy boy, although he suffered from poor health throughout his short life. He developed a love for prayer and began to feel a desire to dedicate himself to God's service. When Gerard was twelve his father died, so the boy had to leave school and work to help support the family. He began to study the art of tailoring, but his employer, a surly man, often treated Gerard badly. Gerard dealt with his situation with great maturity and Christian love.

After completing his training as a tailor, Gerard found work in the house of the bishop of Lacedonia. The young man's desire to serve God grew more intense, and three times he asked to enter a local monastery as a religious brother. But each time the monks refused his request because of his fragile health.

Gerard found his chance to pursue his dream when a band of Redemptorist missionaries preached a mission in Muro. Gathering his courage, he went to the superior and asked to enter the order, but the superior, Fr. Cafaro, said that Gerard's health prevented it. That didn't stop Gerard. He followed the priests as they left the town, running after Fr. Cafaro until he relented and gave Gerard permission to enter their monastery at Iliceto. The priest gave Gerard a note to bring to the superior that read: "I am sending you a useless brother."

Gerard dedicated himself to God completely, not holding anything back. His life became a continual prayer while he carried out ordinary duties with great love. He served as a doorkeeper for the monastery and never turned anyone away. Word soon spread about the brother who would help everyone who asked, and on some days as many as 200 people knocked at the monastery door. Gerard also faced great trials, such as slander and misunderstanding, but he did not let these discourage him.

The gifts of the Holy Spirit gave Gerard a wisdom beyond his years, and he served as spiritual director for several communities of sisters. Gerard also had a charismatic gift of healing, especially for expectant mothers and their unborn children. On one occasion he interceded for a woman facing serious complications during childbirth, and the crisis passed and she gave birth to a healthy child. As Gerard's reputation for holiness spread, people sought him out, asking him to pray for their needs. Many women received graces for themselves and for their children through Gerard's prayers during his life. But after his death even more healings were attributed to his intercession, so Gerard became known as the patron saint of mothers. He is also often invoked by couples experiencing infertility.

After contracting tuberculosis, Gerard died in 1755 at the age of 29. Pope St. Pius X canonized him on December 11, 1904. Gerard's feastday is October 16.

## *Morning Prayer*

*M*orning prayer is a time to give praise and thanks to God, to remind ourselves that he is the source of all beauty and goodness. Lifting one's heart and mind to God in the early hours of the day puts one's life into perspective: God is our loving Creator who watches over us with tenderness and is always ready to embrace us with his compassion and mercy.

While at prayer, try to create a prayerful atmosphere, perhaps with a burning candle to remind you that Christ is the light who illumines your daily path, an open Bible to remind you that the Lord is always present, a crucifix to remind you of the depths of God's love for you. Soft music can also contribute to a serene and prayerful mood.

If a quiet place is not available, or if you pray as you commute to and from work, remember that the God who loves you is present everywhere and hears your prayer no matter the setting.

I will bless the Lord at all times.
His praise will be ever on my lips.

Glory to the Father, and to the Son, and to the
Holy Spirit,
As it was in the beginning, is now, and will be
forever. Amen.

---

## Psalm 27

*Trust in the Lord's loving care.*

With the LORD as my light and my salvation,
who can I fear?
With the LORD as my life's stronghold,
of whom can I be afraid?
Should an army encamp against me,
my heart would not fear;
should war rage against me,
even then would I keep trusting.
One thing have I asked of the LORD,
this have I desired:
that I may dwell in the house of the LORD
all the days of my life,
gazing on the goodness of the LORD
and seeking guidance in his Temple.
Glory to the Father....

—————◆—————

## Psalm 18
*I love you, Lord, my strength.*

The LORD is my stronghold, my fortress, my rescuer,
my God is my rock where I take refuge.
He is my shield, my saving power, my mainstay.
I call on the LORD, worthy of all praise,
and I am saved from my enemies.
In my distress, I called to the LORD and
from his temple my God heard my voice;
my cry came to his presence, to his very ears.
This is why I will praise you, LORD,
    among the nations,
and sing psalms to your name.
Glory to the Father....

—————◆—————

## The Word of God          Isaiah 43:1–4

*The Lord loved us unconditionally, long before we ever loved him. His love is greater than the turmoil in the world; his love is greater than the difficulties we may face.*

This is what the LORD says—Fear not, for I have redeemed you: I have called you by name; you are mine. When you pass through the waters I will be with you, and when you pass through the rivers they will not sweep over you. When you walk through the fire, you will not be burned. For I am the LORD your God, the Holy One of Israel, your Savior. You are precious and honored in my sight and I love you.

*Open my heart to the power of your word.*

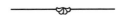

*From prayer one draws the strength needed to meet the challenges of daily life as a committed follower of Jesus Christ, and as such to be a living sign of the Lord's loving presence in the world.*

## Intercessions

**L**ord, I thank you for having gifted me with the light of a new day. Trusting in your promise to be with us and care for our needs, I place my petitions before you and pray:

**Response: *Lord, lead me in your love.***

Open the eyes of my heart to the beauty and goodness that surround me, so that I may see your loving Providence at work in the events of this day. **R.**

Inspire my thoughts, words and actions today, so that all I do and say may be pleasing to you and serve your kingdom here on earth. **R.**

Give me strength to be patient with myself and loving with my family, so that I may be a living witness of your love. **R.**

Be with me today so that I may recognize the opportunities you give me to reach out to others in your name. **R.**

Watch over my loved ones, especially *(name)*, and keep them from harm today, so that when we are reunited this evening we may praise your goodness to us. **R.**

Grant that this family may live in harmony with one another today, so that with one heart we may give glory to your name and witness to your love. **R.**

*(Add your own general intentions and your particular intentions for this novena.)*

*Conclude your intercessions by praying to our Heavenly Father in the words Jesus taught us:*

*Our Father,* who art in heaven, hallowed be thy name; thy kingdom come; thy will be done on earth as it is in heaven. Give us this day our daily bread, and forgive us our trespasses, as we forgive those who trespass against us, and lead us not into temptation, but deliver us from evil. Amen.

## Closing Prayer

*F*ather in heaven, hear my morning prayer and let the splendor of your love light my way. Grant that I may spend this day in joy of spirit and peace of mind. I ask this through Christ, your Son. Amen.

Let us praise the Lord
And give him thanks.

# Novena to St. Gerard

## First Day

### For the Gift of Prayer

*Ask! And it will be given to you; seek! and you shall find; knock! and it shall be opened to you. For everyone who asks, receives; and whoever seeks will find; and to those who knock it shall be opened* (Lk 11:9–10).

St. Gerard, your love of prayer led you to live in close union with God here on earth, and gained for you the happiness of heaven. Teach me to pray with a humble and confident heart, steadfast in trust, so that my prayers may be acceptable to the Lord.

Help me to understand more deeply the spiritual benefits gained by regular participation at Mass and frequent reception of the sacraments. Remind me to turn to God often during the day to praise his power and goodness, to thank him for his countless blessings, to ask for the graces I need most, and to express sorrow for the times I have offended him. Amen.

---

## Novena Prayer

*St. Gerard,* you loved God and served him faithfully while on earth. Now from heaven teach me to have great confidence in the Lord and to recognize his faithful love in my life.

Trusting in your powerful intercession before the most Blessed Trinity, I ask you to obtain this favor *(mention your request).* I believe there is no limit to what God can do, and I place my faith in his infinite wisdom and goodness, always at work even when I cannot see or understand it. I ask you to guide me along life's journey until the day I will join you and all the angels and saints in heaven to praise God for all eternity. Amen.

*Our Father,* who art in heaven, hallowed be thy name; thy kingdom come; thy will be done on earth as it is in heaven. Give us this day our daily bread, and forgive us our trespasses, as we forgive those who trespass against us, and lead us not into temptation, but deliver us from evil. Amen.

---

*Hail Mary,* full of grace, the Lord is with you. Blessed are you among women, and blessed is the fruit of your womb, Jesus. Holy Mary, Mother of God, pray for us sinners, now and at the hour of our death. Amen.

---

*Glory to the Father,* and to the Son, and to the Holy Spirit, as it was in the beginning, is now, and will be forever. Amen.

---

*St. Gerard,* pray for us.

## Second Day

### For the Gift of Trust

*For where your treasure is, there your heart will be, too (Lk 12:34).*

St. Gerard, so often I do not leave room for God in my life. I forget that I can find the Lord even in small things, and that he is with me in all the events of my day. Help me to leave aside the useless worries and anxieties that disturb my inner peace. Pray for me that I may learn to focus on the things that really matter. Teach me how to trust in God and cooperate with him in carrying out his loving plan for my life and the lives of those whom I love.

*(Recite the novena prayer.)*

## Third Day

### For the Gift of Patience

*So I urge you to conduct yourselves in a manner worthy of the calling to which you have been called, with humility, gentleness, and patience. Bear with one another in love… (Eph 4:1–2).*

$S$t. Gerard, help me to be patient with myself and with others, especially... (*my children, spouse, family members, neighbors, coworkers*). Teach me how to accept without resentment the crosses that life brings my way. I ask you to obtain for me the wisdom to know which trials are not for my greater good, and which are in accord with God's design. Show me how to transform these sufferings and use them to grow in holiness, reminding me that Jesus is with me always, even in the unpleasant circumstances of life.

(*Recite the novena prayer.*)

---

*Fourth Day*

## For the Gift of Discipleship

*Let us not grow tired of doing good, for in due time we will also reap a harvest if we do not give up* (Gal 6:9).

$S$t. Gerard, help me to serve the Lord more generously. I want to be wholehearted in following Jesus, giving myself in fitting service to others as he did: family, church and neighborhood community, the workplace.

Help me to understand that humble and loving service, like that of Jesus, can free me from sin and selfishness. If I become discouraged and think that my efforts for God's kingdom may be in vain, speak to my heart the words that Jesus spoke to his disciples: "Let your light so shine before others that they will see your good works and glorify your Father in heaven" (Mt 5:16). May my life always reflect the reality of Christ's life within me. Amen.

*(Recite the novena prayer.)*

---

*Fifth Day*

## For the Gift of Reverence

*I am the bread of life; whoever comes to me shall not hunger, and whoever believes in me shall never thirst* (Jn 6:35).

St. Gerard, awaken in me a profound and living faith in the mystery of the Eucharist, so that when I kneel before the Blessed Sacrament, I will be aware of the Lord's Real Presence.

Help me to better appreciate the great gift of the Holy Eucharist. I pray for the gift of reverence, that I may love the Lord with all my heart, offer him fitting worship and praise him for everything he has given to me. May my reception of the Eucharist transform me so that my life will invite others to walk with the Lord and follow his way. Amen.

*(Recite the novena prayer.)*

## Sixth Day

### For the Gift of Forgiveness

*For if you forgive others their offenses, your Heavenly Father will forgive you too; but if you do not forgive others, neither will your Father forgive your offenses (Mt 6:14–16).*

St. Gerard, help me to live the spirit of the Our Father, to forgive injuries as I want others to forgive me when I offend them. When past hurts come to mind, help me to forgive again, deep within my heart, so I can finally be free of anger, bitterness and the desire for revenge.

Show me how to be an instrument of the Lord's peace and love within my family, among my friends and neighbors, coworkers and colleagues. I pray that my heart may be a worthy dwelling place for the Holy Spirit, and my life a witness to the healing power of Jesus. Amen.

*(Recite the novena prayer.)*

## Seventh Day

### For the Gift of Right Judgment

*Foster that love which flows from a pure heart, a clean conscience and sincere faith (1 Tm 1:5).*

St. Gerard, ask the Lord to grant me the grace of right judgment so that I may know God's plan for my life and the lives of those whom I love. Help me to rely on Divine Wisdom to make conscientious choices following the path of God's law.

For those times when I choose not to walk along the path of virtue, teach me to repent and approach the Sacrament of Reconciliation with great confidence in the Lord's mercy. Ask him to grant me a humble heart to recognize my sinfulness and my need for forgiveness. Amen.

*(Recite the novena prayer.)*

## Eighth Day

### For the Gift of a Generous Spirit

*On the third day there was a wedding in Cana of Galilee, and Jesus' mother was there. Now Jesus was also invited to the wedding as well as his disciples, and when the wine ran out Jesus' mother said to him, "They have no wine." Jesus replied, "What do you want from me, woman? My hour has not come yet." His mother said to the servants, "Do whatever he tells you"* (Jn 2:1–5).

St. Gerard, I ask you to obtain for me the gift of joyful self-giving. Help me to understand that I can find genuine happiness as I do my best to care for my family.

During your life you found in Mary a source of comfort and a secure guide in all the events of your life. Teach me to turn to her in trust and confidence when I feel the weight of family responsibilities, when I feel that others ask more of me than I can give. Like Mary, God's Mother and mine, let me know the joy that comes in living my life for others. Amen.

*(Recite the novena prayer.)*

---

## Ninth Day

### For the Gift of Hope

*Come, you blessed of my Father, receive the kingdom prepared for you from the foundation of the world* (Mt 25:34).

*S*t. Gerard, the Church has raised you up as a witness to holiness of life and as a reminder of our own destiny. I ask you to be a friend and guide to me as I follow the Lord and do my best to draw others to his love. If I grow weary along my journey to heaven, remind me of my own call to holiness, and the reward of everlasting life promised to those who follow the Lord wholeheartedly. Amen.

*(Recite the novena prayer.)*

# Prayers for Various Needs

### Prayer for Motherhood

St. Gerard, powerful intercessor before God, I come to ask your help. Beseech the Lord, the Giver of all life, to grant me the grace to conceive a child, if it be according to his plan. I hope to bear children who will be faith-filled disciples of Jesus, witnesses to his message of love, and heirs to the kingdom of heaven. Amen.

---

### Prayer for an Expectant Mother

Almighty and loving God, through the power of the Holy Spirit you prepared the Virgin Mary to be the worthy bearer of your own Son, Jesus. Listen to my prayer through the intercession of St. Gerard, your faithful servant, and protect (name) during her pregnancy and birthing.

Creator of Life, grant (name) the joy of anticipating new life within her womb, and in time of pain or distress allow her to experience your consoling presence. Grant her, Lord, the spiritual and emotional care she needs in order to bring her child into the world. Give (name) the wisdom to know how to safeguard her physical welfare so that the child she carries within her may be healthy in mind and body. May all of her children bring her joy and reflect your love for her until they may, one day, enjoy the eternal happiness of heaven. Amen.

―――――――― ❧ ――――――――

## An Expectant Mother's Prayer

Almighty and loving God, through the power of the Holy Spirit you prepared the Virgin Mary to be the worthy bearer of your Son, Jesus. Listen to my prayer through the intercession of St. Gerard, your faithful servant, and watch over me during my pregnancy and birthing.

Creator of Life, grant (husband's name) and me the joy of anticipating new life within my womb, and in time of pain or distress let me experience your consoling presence. Grant me good judgment to seek the spiritual and emotional support I need to bring our child into the world. Give me the wisdom to know how to safeguard my physical welfare so that the child I carry within me may be healthy in mind and body. Teach me how to be a loving wife and a devoted mother so that our children may bring us joy and witness to your love until we all, one day, enjoy the eternal happiness of heaven. Amen.

---

## A Husband's Prayer

Almighty and loving God, through the power of the Holy Spirit you prepared the Virgin Mary to be the worthy bearer of your Son, Jesus. Listen to my prayer through the intercession of St. Gerard, your faithful servant, and protect (*name*) during her pregnancy and birthing.

Creator of Life, grant us the joy of anticipating together the new life within her womb, and in time of pain or distress show me how to comfort and cherish her. Grant me, Lord, the wisdom to know how to help (*name*) in her special needs at this time. Safeguard her physical and emotional well-being so that our child will be healthy in mind and body. Give me courage that I may willingly accept the responsibility of raising children, and grant me a generous heart that I may find joy even in self-sacrifice to provide for their needs. Teach me how to be a loving husband and a devoted father so that our children may bring us joy and witness to your love until we all, one day, enjoy the eternal happiness of heaven. Amen.

---

## A Married Couple's Prayer

St. Gerard, powerful intercessor before God, we come to ask your help. Beseech the Lord, the Giver of all life, to grant us the grace to bring new life into the world if it be according to his will. We desire and hope to be co-creators in God's plan of creation, to raise children who will be faith-filled disciples of Jesus, witnesses to his message of love and heirs to the kingdom of heaven. Amen.

---

## Prayer of Praise and Thanksgiving

*It is fitting for us to praise and thank God for the graces and privileges he has bestowed upon the saints. Devotees of St. Gerard may pray the following act of thanksgiving during their novena.*

*L*ord Jesus, I praise, glorify and bless you for all the graces and privileges you have bestowed upon your chosen servant and friend, Gerard Majella. By his merits grant me your grace, and through his intercession help me in all my needs. At the hour of my death be with me until that time when I can join the saints in heaven to praise you forever and ever. Amen.

## Evening Prayer

As this day draws to a close we place ourselves in an attitude of thanksgiving. We take time to express our gratitude to a loving God for his abiding presence. We thank him for the gift of the day and all it brought with it. We thank him for all the things we were able to achieve throughout the day, and we entrust to him the concerns we have for tomorrow.

From the rising to the setting of the sun,
May the name of the Lord be praised.
Glory to the Father, and to the Son, and to the
Holy Spirit,
As it was in the beginning, is now, and will be
forever. Amen.

Take a few moments for a brief examination of conscience. Reflect on the ways God acted in your life today, how you responded to his invitations to think, speak and act in a more Christlike manner, and in what ways you would like to be a more faithful disciple tomorrow.

For the times I failed to be generous and loving
toward my spouse and children.

*Jesus, Good Shepherd, have mercy.*

For the times I was moody, sullen and unresponsive.

*Jesus, Good Shepherd, have mercy.*

For the times I was untruthful, unforgiving,
resentful.

*Jesus, Good Shepherd, have mercy.*

For the times...(any other petitions for pardon).
(Or any other Act of Sorrow.)

## Psalm 23

*Our God is good, his love is eternal.*

The LORD is my shepherd;
nothing do I want.
He makes me lie down in verdant pastures,
he guides me along soothing streams.
He refreshes my soul.
He leads me along paths of righteousness
for the sake of his name.
Even though I walk in the dark valley
I fear no evil,
because you are with me.
Your rod and your staff give me courage.
You spread the table before me

in the face of my foes;
you have anointed my head with oil;
my cup overflows.
May only contentment and loving kindness
be with me all the days of my life,
and may I dwell in the house of the LORD
    for years to come.
Glory to the Father....

---

## The Word of God  John 3:16–17

*God created us for himself, and he wants to share his divine life with us here on earth and in the eternal happiness of heaven. The Lord wants our salvation more than we ourselves could want it.*

For God so loved the world that he gave his only-begotten Son, so that everyone who believed in him would not die but have eternal life. For God did not send his Son into the world to judge the world, but so the world would be saved through him.

*Your words, Lord, give joy to my heart!*

---

*In prayer we bring before the Lord our own needs and the needs of those we love. We take time to consider the needs of the world and intercede for those who do not or cannot pray. We offer petitions for the improvement of the human condition so that our world will be a better place to live, and all people may contribute to building up God's kingdom here on earth.*

## Intercessions

*F*ather in heaven, we thank you for the gifts you have given us today. With confidence in your loving care, we offer our needs to you and the needs of your people.

**Response: *Receive our prayer through the intercession of St. Gerard.***

Inspire leaders of governments to enact laws that protect life at every stage and foster respect for peoples of all cultures. **R.**

Grant wisdom and compassion to those who minister in your name. **R.**

Console and support all mothers who endure any discomforts from pregnancy and childbirth. **R.**

Give expectant parents the joy of anticipating the birth of their child, and the confident understanding that they are co-creators with you. **R.**

Grant to all expectant mothers the spiritual, material and emotional support they need to bring their children into this world. **R.**

Transform the hearts of all those who may be considering abortion because of shame, fear, poverty or inconvenience. **R.**

Heal the hearts of all those who have sought abortion as a solution and now endure the emotional trauma of its aftermath. **R.**

Encourage and strengthen single parents who do their best to face the countless challenges of raising their children. **R.**

Grant the gift of patience and fertility to married couples who want to conceive a child. **R.**

Give to all mothers and fathers the love, wisdom and courage they need to form their children as disciples of your Son. **R.**

Comfort the sick and the dying; welcome all who have died into the joy of heaven. **R.**

*(Add any other spontaneous intentions and your particular intentions for this novena.)*

*Conclude your intercessions by praying to our Heavenly Father in the words Jesus taught us:*

Our Father, who art in heaven....

## Closing Prayer

*G*racious Lord, receive our evening prayer. Guard us from evil and bring us safely through the night, so that with the coming of a new day we may serve you more faithfully. We ask this through Christ, your Son, our Lord. Amen.

*Mary, Jesus' Mother and ours, is always ready to intercede for those who ask her help.*

Hail, Holy Queen, Mother of mercy, our life, our sweetness and our hope! To you we cry, poor banished children of Eve. To you we send up our sighs, mourning and weeping in this valley of tears. Turn then, most gracious advocate, your eyes of mercy toward us, and after this our exile, show to us the blessed fruit of your womb, Jesus. O clement, O loving, O sweet Virgin Mary.

May God's blessing remain with us forever. In the name of the Father, and of the Son, and of the Holy Spirit. Amen.

# BOOKS & MEDIA

The Daughters of St. Paul operate book and media centers at the following addresses. Visit, call, or write the one nearest you today, or find us at www.pauline.org.

**CALIFORNIA**
3908 Sepulveda Blvd, Culver City, CA 90230    310-397-8676
935 Brewster Avenue, Redwood City, CA 94063    650-369-4230
5945 Balboa Avenue, San Diego, CA 92111    858-565-9181

**FLORIDA**
145 S.W. 107th Avenue, Miami, FL 33174    305-559-6715

**HAWAII**
1143 Bishop Street, Honolulu, HI 96813    808-521-2731
Neighbor Islands call:    866-521-2731

**ILLINOIS**
172 North Michigan Avenue, Chicago, IL 60601    312-346-4228

**LOUISIANA**
4403 Veterans Memorial Blvd, Metairie, LA 70006    504-887-7631

**MASSACHUSETTS**
885 Providence Hwy, Dedham, MA 02026    781-326-5385

**MISSOURI**
9804 Watson Road, St. Louis, MO 63126    314-965-3512

**NEW YORK**
64 W. 38th Street, New York, NY 10018    212-754-1110

**PENNSYLVANIA**
Philadelphia—relocating    215-676-9494

**SOUTH CAROLINA**
243 King Street, Charleston, SC 29401    843-577-0175

**VIRGINIA**
1025 King Street, Alexandria, VA 22314    703-549-3806

**CANADA**
3022 Dufferin Street, Toronto, ON M6B 3T5    416-781-9131

¡También somos su fuente para libros,
videos y música en español!